Broken
Heart

Broken Heart

100 Poems
By Lily Joy Isaac

LUMINARY PUBLISHING HOUSE

For permissions or licensing inquiries, please contact: Luminary Publishing House, LLC at inquire@luminarypublishinghouse.com

ISBN (Paperback): 978-1-968972-00-4
ISBN (eBook): 978-1-968972-01-1
ISBN (Hardcover): 978-1-968972-02-8

Luminary Publishing House, LLC
https://luminarypublishinghouse.com

Cover Design by Julsiji Julsiji.wordpress.com

LUMINARY PUBLISHING HOUSE

Playlist

Conan Gray - Family Line

Tom Odell - Black Friday

Shaya Zamora - Cigarette

Billie Eilish - The 30th

SYML - Where's My Love

sombr - undressed

Conan Gray - Heather

Lana Del Rey - Young And Beautiful

NF - Trauma

Lizzy McAlpine - doomsday

Tom Odell - Can't Pretend

Billie Eilish - WILDFLOWER

Harry Styles - Sign of the Times

James Arthur - Car's Outside

The Neighbourhood - Reflections

Alex Warren - Burning Down

Lorde - Writer In The Dark

NF - Time - Edit

Cigarettes After Sex - Cry

New West - Those Eyes - Sped Up

Billie Eilish - Your Power

NF - Remember This

Bruno Mars - Grenade

Mitski - A Pearl

Tom Odell - Just Another Thing We Don't Talk About

Mitski - Me and My Husband

Michael Jackson - Earth Song

Lady Gaga,Bruno Mars - Die With A Smile

Halsey - Sorry

Tom Odell - Sirens

Robbie Williams,Carter J. Murphy,Steve Pemberton - Feel (From Better Man

Mazzy Star - Fade Into You

Gorillaz - Rhinestone Eyes

GoodBooks,Crystal Castles - Leni (Crystal Castles vs GoodBooks)

Ladytron – Seventeen

David Kunshhner – Daylight

Open 🟢 | Search 🔍 | Scan 📷

Table of Contents

Heart   *1*

   Emotions   2

   What awaits me outside of this flower shop?   3

   In school you imagine friendships to be forever   4

   Love for a sinner   6

   Crying   7

   Forever and always,   8

   Seventeen and Single   9

   Death   10

   Be Yourself   12

   Broken heart   13

   I want to be loved   14

   You wish you'd listened   15

   Pretty privilege   17

   The worst part   19

   Unspoken rules   20

   Growing up   21

   We never dated   22

   Expectations   23

   Sadness   24

   Validation   25

   Sacrifice   26

   I thought you were my best friend   27

   My heart is made of glass   28

   Twice in your life   29

   Resentment is like a vine   30

   Beauty   31

Pen to paper   32

Hurt   *33*

The blade   34

Seasonal self-sabotage   35

Coping mechanisms   36

Overthinking   37

We Have Matching tattoos   38

Intrusive thoughts   39

Nails   40

Sadness unlocked   41

I'm not suicidal   42

Mistakes   43

Wounded   44

Rage fuels the rifle   45

Escapism is a tree   46

Addiction   47

Hurting in silence   48

Fitting in   49

Self-sabotage   50

Death   52

I'm Going Deeper   53

Problems   54

Oblivious   55

Silhouette   56

Branded   57

Living to survive   58

My plans   59

Hate   *60*

There's a Demon Living In my mind   61

Proof of my hate for you   62

Guilt   63

I am the demon   65

You ruined me   66

Pink   67

What was once the truth   68

Goodbye   69

Comparison is the Thief of Joy   70

Cigarette   71

Locked and Loaded   72

Suffocation   73

Not really proud   74

God says   75

Society pretty   76

Don't take it personally   77

I don't trust happiness   78

Do I hate myself?   79

Manipulator   80

Insane   82

Closed eyes   83

Control   84

A Sword is a Weapon of War   85

To be loved by a writer   86

Fame is just a game   87

Hollow   *89*

Devils' waters   90

Betrayal   92

Acceptance is my Muse   93

Dicentra   94

Stranger   95

Fear   97

Attachment 98

Anxiety 99

Denial 100

Ghosted 101

Do I trust you? 102

Secrets 103

Silver 104

Tears 105

Walking away 106

Another life 107

Haunted 108

Homesick 109

The backup friend 110

Society's cell 111

Cannot feel any rest 112

Difficult to love 113

Museum of memories 114

Acknowledgements 116

My Testimony 117

Author Bio 120

To those who feel too much and receive too little.

To Jesus, who heals my hurt.

Heart

I put my heart and my soul into my work and have lost my mind in the process.

— Vincent Van Gogh

Emotions

As kids we are conditioned to speak through our emotions.
Our cries became explosions and
Parents hurriedly try to keep us quiet.
Once we hit teenage years we become compliant,
No longer being reliant on the ones
Who raised us.
Our faces become blank
Like a piece of wood waiting to be carved.
Yet, deep down, we are anything but clean and unmarked.
We become equivalent to mud—
A stain on a clean shirt—
Seen as too much.
Once we grew up people questioned,
Their faces perplexed at the idea of us,
Keeping it together. Although we've been doing it forever,
Not realising it started shortly after birth,
When we were hushed at the back of an auditorium,
Our parents praying to feel euphoria,
At the cost of our sensoria.

What awaits me outside of this flower shop?

My body is wrapped in paper,
As the shop bell rings.
I am passed from your hands,
Into the hands of another,

The shop bell rings again from afar;
I don't know what anticipates me.
Is it a new piece of paper,
Or is it a vase filled with vapour?

Since I was plucked from the field,
I've never known which path
I'd be forced to follow.
Perhaps I'd be placed somewhere filled with pain,

With my leaves cut off and my petals drooping.
Perhaps my life will be looping.

In school you imagine friendships to be forever

With each traded text I felt fear.
I planned to spend the hours beyond school
Emitting the essence of enjoyment,

After our subdued speech,
We let silence plan our days apart.
It was never voiced, yet everyone was afraid,
Fearing the person who you'd call the "governor" of the group.

Slithering her way into the group,
She manipulated the majority.
Except me, I was playing her game.
Simply because I couldn't be bothered anymore.

She slowly but successfully manipulated everyone—
Made them think she was perfect—
She'd create arguments out of air
To make everybody look bad and to make herself look brilliant.

The manipulation she did was unmatched.
She played her cards right.
She'd tricked everyone under the sun,
All her old friend groups, yet, I still had a full deck.

She would make you think that they had wronged her,
But in reality, she had wronged them,
She had wronged us all.
No one could see the truth except me.

I could discern the evil from the good.
There were two bad people in the group,
But the lesser of the two had been humbled quickly
After the primary manipulator, again, had made an argument.

Why did she do this? You might ask.
She was insecure, and she wanted control.
She wanted to make herself feel like the best.
This terrible technique might last in high school.

But it won't last long,
It certainly won't last eternally.

Love for a sinner

"Is there any love for a sinner?" The girl asked the Lord.

"Of course, there is," He replied.

"But how can there be, when I've as good as murdered the boy?"

She argued, remembering the pain she's caused him.

Before he could reply, she continued to speak. "After everything I've done,

How can you forgive me?"

The Lord smiled before replying, "When you understand

The depth of suffering that my son had to go through for you—

His organs were seen. There was no skin left for him to bear."

The Lord weeped as he remembered the suffering.

The realisation hit her, about sly Satan's deceptive sounds

Whispering in her ear over and over again,

"You're worthless. You've committed too many sins.

God would never forgive you."

The lies she listened to. The words she worshiped

As if they were the truth.

When the being she should've listened to

Was sitting right in front of her.

The girl weeped just as Jesus did

All those years ago, when he was hung on the cross,

His organs exposed, and his health declining,

But he held onto the Holy Spirit,

Knowing he would rise again,

By the power of the Glorious God.

Crying

Tears are a shield between your eyes and the world.
Sometimes when we have nothing left
Crying is the only thing keeping us sane
In those times when we ponder the point of life.

We know it won't make sense to anyone, but
Tears are the only comfort we can receive and
The only protection we're allowed to gain.

In those moments,
Crying is the only act we need.
It's what speaks for us when our mouths refrain.

Forever and always,

That's what we said.
Yet words aren't always
Taken literally.
People say the truth hurts.

When we broke up,
It was like the ocean,
Which you'd removed,
Came back over me.

I began to drown once more
As I realised
It wasn't really forever
Was it?

Seventeen and Single

Like a ladybug in a web full of flies,
You conform with the crowd and I
Resist the rules.

You abandon your allies and become loyal to your lover,
I fix to my friends and deny the idea of fraternising with another.

I'm seventeen and still single,
Content with being contrary to conformity.
Is your teenage romance worth the pain?
Or perhaps you'll end up with lifelong gain.

Does your romance remain,
Or do one of you refrain?
Once I reach the top of my teenage years,
Do I gain the ecstatic enchantment

Of a teenage romance?
Or do I stay single but no longer seventeen?

Death

The boy stood as death stared him in the eye
And said, "You've not lived enough yet."
Death smiled a sickly smile,
Thinking about the different types of pain
this boy was about to endure:

The death of his mother,
The grief of his father,
The betrayal of his brother,
And the heartbreak of losing himself,

As the boy was caught up in the pain,
He slowly lost himself.
The grip his hands had on his own soul
Slowly slipped into a hole,
And death grabbed a hold of him,
It was too late for the boy to rescue himself
From the power which death possessed.
His consciousness was crushed;
Oxygen no longer entered his lungs.
His funeral, which he expected to have a multitude of people,
Was almost empty.
They say an average of 50 people attend your funeral
Depending on the weather.
The mouth of the church closed and no more than 50 people entered
The hall with only 10 of those people having truly known
The boy who was defeated by death.

On his day of death, the boy wondered how many

Would be at his funeral.

It was definitely meant to be more than this.

The amount of people who show up tells you who truly cares,

But what about the people who don't show up?

They'll give a pathetic excuse as to why.

People move on with their lives:

They'll forget about the boy.

But when the boy stood as death stared him in the eye,

In the midst of the eternal fiery furnace,

He said to death, "You won."

Be Yourself

It's what we were all told,
But what was once the truth became a lie
After I discovered the fear of being judged.
People would look me in the eye,
"You're so pretty," they would say.
When in reality they thought I only looked okay, I realised.
Hearing my name whispered in the shadows,
Their sharpened arrows were no longer disguised.

Fear engulfed me
Like the vast waves in the sea.
So, I stopped listening to outdated advice.
Instead, I created my own rules to suffice.

I lived by these regulations,
Forging illustrations of my life,
Ignoring the aspirations of others
Over my desires for this life
All because I no longer listened
To the prehistoric protocols
Of social serendipity.

Broken heart

Born with a broken heart,
Living as a natural target,
I'm hit with a dart of dark emotions and
Each one feels extreme.

Droplets of black ink pour into the book of my broken heart.
Each word spills onto the piece of paper just like art.
A new emotion, a separate situation.
It hurts to let go, yet there's no deviation.

It's taken me too long to understand,
That they don't care how much I'm hurting,
Even though with my broken heart,
I still keep on searching.

My heart needs healing,
My secrets need revealing,
And I need to pull out the dart
Lodged into my broken heart.

I want to be loved

I'm terrified of being known.
As you peel away the layers of my personality
And open each door of my character,

What if you don't like me?
Will you slowly start to resent me?
Do the little things I do annoy you and
Will you leave me like they did?

Will I ever take the risk?
I wonder if I will ever even be loved.
I'm terrified, yet I want to be known.

You wish you'd listened

When you enter the restaurant on the first date,
He pulls out the chair for you.
You smile, thinking he's a gentleman.
By the third date you become fond of his familiar touch,
In love with his personality.
The day he asks you to be his girlfriend
Climbs to the top five of the best days of your life
Now that you're finally learning to be treated right.
Since, in the past, relationships were a hard task,
In front of friends, I always wore a mask.
You think of the future, imagining one with him in it.
But Love is like a fox.
A few months in, you observe how he treats others with unkindness.
Ignoring the red flags, you stay in the relationship.
No matter what people tell you,
You don't listen,
Blinded by the feeling of falling in love.
Your wedding day is the best day of your life.
A month into the marriage, he acts like the best husband,
"See," you tell people.
"It's the honeymoon phase," they say,
Not letting you justify what's unknowingly going to come.
Six months in he shouts, blaming you for things which aren't your fault.
He's had a stressful day, you justify,
Not knowing it'll get worse.
A year in, he throws a glass at you.
That's when you realise, they were right.
He'd stripped away your self-worth.
Each time the clear skies became a storm

15

You held your breath, hoping that one day he'd go back
to being the man you once knew,
He never did.

Pretty privilege

"Pretty privilege isn't real," they say.
But if I didn't have blonde straight hair,
I would have a societal disadvantage,
And become an outcast,
Because I would not be like everyone else.

The desire to be pretty carves out damage—
More than a bullet ever could.
"If you lost some weight, you'd be pretty."
"If you gained some weight, you'd look better."
"You should straighten your hair."
"You should cut your hair, it's too long."

The true meaning of the word, in our world,
Implies that if you fit into society's mass produced
Standards it would make it easier—
Easier for them to sell to you and
Faster for them to influence you.

Buy that product.
Cut your hair like that!
Diet to look like those models
Who've paid millions for plastic surgery.
Destroy your mental health!
Pay for therapy.
Get married and have kids!
Oh, now that you've done that,
Your body isn't perceived as nice.
You've looked after the kids, so,

Start up your career once more.

All of these voices, influencing me
To follow these beauty standards,
The same people who caved—
The ones who were never an outcast.
The voices of the ones who have pretty privilege.

The worst part

I let myself be delusional,
Staying in the same space.
Deep down I knew it would never happen,
I knew that this wasn't my lane,
But I pretended it was.

That was the worst part—
It was the wickedest part.
It's like a rock that's trying to stay afloat,
But the weight is just too much.
As much as I might love you,

I know it will never work,
Not everyone who's entered my life is meant to stay,
And now I have to obey.
All that's left are the memories of you and me.
No matter how tightly I hold on,
You will always leave.

Unspoken rules

As children we are taught to follow rules,
"Keep in line, one behind the other."
"Don't get lost. Stick to your brother."
But as soon as we step one foot out of place,
Any space we had becomes invaded,
As well as the removal of any grace.
As we get older, we learn
Of the unspoken rules of society.
We begin to embrace any feelings of compliancy:
"It's simple," they say.
Go to university, get a job, find a nice place to stay.
Conditioning us to push any creativity to the back of our minds,
They don't encourage us to have any time to unwind.
By the time we're adults we have regulations
Under the impression that it's too late,
We can no longer ignore the bait.
Yet we feel unable to express any creativity,
No longer having access to the ability
Of artistry, just as we realise
It may be too late.
After chasing the rulebook,
We gained little in exchange for time they took.

Growing up

As you grow up, you begin to realise
That everything you were ever told was a lie.

They watch as you stand by,
Unable to find a job.
"Get an education," they said,
Now you're scrolling for a job,
Each application rejected,
Yet you still apply for the next.

In high school they told you it would be your peak,
Except everyone thought you were a freak.
You didn't have many friends,
Unlike what the movies prophesied.

Reality differed from your expectations,
And now you have to pay.

We never dated

Why did I cry over a guy
Who hadn't even cracked open a window
Into the depths of my soul?

He stole space in my mind,
Living there rent free,
While his thoughts were the opposite of me.

Why did I dream of someone who didn't feel the same?
Perhaps this was all a game and
I was being tricked by my brain.

Having a crush is such a pain.
Yet it's almost impossible to forget
The dreams and destinations,

That I wanted to achieve.
But of course,
It was all an expectation,
Contrary to what my dreams had baited.

Expectations

It never would've worked out.
The expectations were tight,
And she was right,
Her standards were higher than this.

She deserved a kiss filled with bliss,
Not a slither of spit.
She deserved a ring,
She didn't want the sting
Of being wrong

Just as she always was.
Except this time, she so badly wanted
To be wrong.
Yet she wasn't, for once in her life,
She was right.

Sadness

When despair drowns upon your heart,
Who hears the torment in your tears?
Do you keep them locked inside
That dark dusty drawer?

The deep feeling of sadness in your chest,
That unexplainable emotion
Which you can't control.
Where do you hide it?

I was told to change my mindset,
But how can I do that
When what I'm changing to is unknown to me?

The sadness is stilling,
I am forced to sit in desolation,
Unable to do anything with it.

This state of constant gloom and grief—
All I feel is sadness—
I can't even cry.

Validation

Is like a shadow
Following me around constantly,
But I can't seem to catch it.
I am resentful of the shadows.
They happily live the path
I am forced to pursue.
Going after the pre-created trail of tragedy,

I am unable to fill the ever-growing void.
Pleasing people gave me validation,
Although as soon as the feeling came
It went straight to the grave,
Walking away, I realised

I will never gain enough praise,
If I continue to stay in a daze,
Of not feeling validated,
And continuing to be ambulated.

Sacrifice

Jesus gave up his life.
That is the biggest sacrifice of all,
The pain spreading throughout his body,
As he was nailed to the cross.
When he was on the cross
He thought of me and you.
He did the will of his father in heaven,
The blood that poured out of his eyes,
As he thought of the suffering he was going to endure.
His flesh which would be whipped,
Leaving his organs to be seen,
The sacrifice he was going to make
For the people he loves—
That is sacrifice.

I thought you were my best friend

I heard your favourite song today,
Through somebody's not so silent headphones.
I remember how fulfilled I'd feel when you'd text me,
"Hey, thanks for today. It was so fun."
In that moment, I felt like I'd found a true best friend.
I was so sure you were the answer to my prayers,
But everything was a lie.
You made me excited to go to school—
The joy of seeing a good friend,
After years and years of failed friendships—
I truly thought you were the one:
The best friend you only gain once in a lifetime,
Yet I couldn't be more wrong.
When as soon as he came along,
He snatched you up,
The girl I once knew was no more.
The bond we'd created in our first few months
Of our friendship dissipated
Into thin air, as if it was never really there.
I began to question if I was imagining it.
Perhaps in my head I'd bent the truth to make it fit.
September turned into November,
And our friendship turned into
Something I could hardly remember.

My heart is made of glass

Time is beginning to pass,
The pieces scattered,
And my heart is shattered.
You left without a goodbye,
Leaving me to stand by.
When I told you I had been broken before,
You helped me to feel restored,
Sealing my cracks with love.
I thought you were an angel from above,
That was, until you came along
Without your usual birdsong
Hitting me with the bane of betrayal.
Looking back this was inevitable.
I just wish I knew,
So that I could've saved my heart from you.

Twice in your life

There's a theory that you'll always meet a person
Twice in your life. Today I met you as if
It was for the first time.
You had a different hair style,
Looking like it hadn't been cut in a while, and
You were taller than I remembered.

We spoke as if we were never apart,
Like this meeting was just the start.
I wish it was over forever.
If only we were never together.

Walking away with a sigh,
I looked back and realised it was all a lie;
It wasn't really you I spoke to.

You didn't give me a kiss,
There were no feelings of bliss,
So maybe you do meet people twice in your life.

But perhaps not the same version,
Of the specific person.

Resentment is like a vine

It climbs my walls,
Binding me to anger, anguish, and pain,
Not allowing me to gain
Restoration or revelation.
I wanted closure,
Wanting and praying for it to be over—
All the past empty promises
Burned in furnaces.
Old memories carved out of lies,
The wood rotting,
The vines bonding,
Trying to cover up the tracks,
Of all the painful cracks,
Which you created,
And now I'm left seething
With resentment.

Beauty

Each of us are given a canvas.
Some fill them with pain and hope,
Others with privilege and happiness.
As our lives go on,
And the canvas is drawn upon,
Sometimes the paint spills,
And our body fills with chills.
As the strokes grow,
The depths of our feelings begin to show, and
The canvas expresses what others will never know.
Some strokes are jagged and splattered,
While others are crisp and neat.
The art of beauty is how well we can mask
The exaggeration of our emotions.
How much concealer can I blend into my skin
Before it becomes too cakey?
When will the canvas of my organs be viewed as pretty?
They say beauty isn't subjective,
Yet if I'm not pretty I'm neglected.
"Everyone is beautiful," they say,
Yet some people have privilege,
Not because of the canvas in their heart,
They still get a jumpstart,
Society judges me based on trends and ends.
Am I beautiful if my canvas is covered
In splatters and jagged strokes?

Pen to paper

Writing creates books which line the shelves
Of my heart. Ink runs through my veins,
As poetry expresses my pain.
Writing is a different kind of art:
Not your typical drawing or painting
But its life changing.
Literature is political and heart-seeking.
It's the voice for those who are unable to speak,

A writer's mind is a war zone:
The constant battle between different characters.
My anger is angelic,
And my problems are picturesque.
Books are an insight into a writer's euphoria.
Characters express the experiences of the author,
Books enable us to skip chapters when life doesn't let us,
They're the escape from reality into fantasy.

Hurt

If you don't deal with your demons, they will deal with you, and it's gonna hurt.

— Nikki Sixx

The blade

Consumes my mind.
The constant thoughts of it,
My desperation for the blood,
For it to penetrate my skin,
To feel it pierce me,
For the blood to appear,
Temporary relief is what I crave.

Families have generational curses,
I've got yearly ones.
June is my month of judgement,
And I'm judging myself.
I deserve this pain,
Jesus took it away,
So now I feel like I have to
Cause myself harm.

Self-harm is like a broken record.
It repeats without stopping— a daily addiction,
And the worst part about it is
I can't feel the difference
Between the guilt now
And the guilt before.
I caved to the temptation
And now crimson liquid drips from my arms,
As the guard to my shame is disarmed.

Seasonal self-sabotage

The destruction in my life
Surfaces depending on the knife.
It might be going great,
Then next thing you know I want to harm myself.
The urge is a constant battle in my mind:
All kinds of ethics departing from inside.
My heart and skin ripping away;
Each layer signifying a new struggle,
Other coping mechanisms aren't quite the same;
They don't fit into the category of my deliberate wounds.
Searching for the feeling through characters in books,
Doesn't scratch the itch,
The ice method,
Doesn't exactly fill the gaping hole,
Which I'm desperately trying to fill
Through seasonal self-sabotage.
I know the answer:
It's tapping into Jesus,
Hearing what he has to offer,
But a small part of me,
Is comfortable in the pain,
Expectant of the pending depression.
A section of me enjoys the blade—
The blood it gifts me.

Coping mechanisms

Bad coping mechanisms are like old familiar friends.
I approach them with the urge to say,
I've not seen you in a while and
Being with you felt good
until it didn't.

I don't deserve to feel the familiar touch.
My life is close to perfect
So, why do I feel this way?
My love for you is like a punch in the gut.
At first it doesn't hurt—
It doesn't make a difference—
But then the pain and guilt surrender
And your presence becomes my reality.

The struggle seemed surreal,
Stuck at the back of my mind,
Until it was all I could think about.
I'm putting my hands up in acceptance
Of my actions from the past that are
Now becoming performances of the present.

Overthinking

Younger me was right:
There are monsters which creep in at night,
Except they aren't under the bed,
They're in my head.

The monsters have taken over.
They control how my brain thinks.
It feels like my mind no longer belongs to me.

My brain picks at things that I've done during the day,
And it effects my sleep at night.
I want to stop it more than anything,
Even if it's a few minutes of peace—
Just a second of heavenly sleep.

It's a constant reminder that I'm not who I want to be:
A light shinning so bright, living the life I desire.
If I was, I wouldn't be thinking about it.
All I want is peace.

Overthinking destroys my sleep,
Were others whispering about me,
Or am I overthinking it?

We Have Matching tattoos

Except this one isn't a normal,
One created by ink and done by a professional,
While this tattoo is a reflection of the hard times in my life.
It's the same one that thousands of people have,
It's made by the release of blood,
Etched into my skin by an amateur,

On average, one out of six people you know
Have this tattoo. It's like a statue on my skin,
Pushing us into exile, like a trial,
We're made to let go of past pain over time,

It started out as a struggle,
But then the feelings became muddled,
No longer any trouble.

We have matching tattoos.
They are a reminder of all the things that went wrong.
My memories of the experience long gone,
Leaving behind the feeling of temporary relief.

Sometimes I want to relive that feeling,
But my healer doesn't deserve a redo
Of the past addiction.
We have matching tattoos,
Some might call them scars.

Intrusive thoughts

The unwelcome echoes in her mind
Haunt her soul with restless whispers.
The girl was walking home.
She had a good day,
Or at least it seemed like she did

On the outside, but in her mind, it was a bad day.
The demons plagued her with whispers
Each second of every hour,
And that's when the unwelcome echoes finally had an effect.
She picked up her feet from the pavement,
Smashing them against the rocky road.
She thought this was finally the end of her life,
But her wishes were not suffice.

Her body collapsed beneath the blue battered Bentley.
The bright light poured into the covers to her soul
A faint beeping continued as the world returned in fragments,
Opening her eyes she was met with blank ceiling tiles,
And her breath continued to be expressed for miles.

Nails

The many ways that we can decorate them:
Different colours and choices,
Nails can be used as a display of beauty
Or to make different things.
The nails that were used to build your bed,
The ones in your wall holding up your picture frames,
But what about the nails that held your saviour to the cross?
The blood covered nails which pierced through Christs' skin,
So much pain he went through all because of us:
The weeping of his own blood,
The world that he loved so deeply that held
All of those people. The same ones who killed him,
They committed regicide on our king,
"If Jesus is really God,
why doesn't he come and show us?"
People sometimes ask. Yet they don't realise
He did, and we killed him.

Sadness unlocked

People say that anger is a cover up.
Now that I'm no longer angry
Sadness has been unlocked.

The face others see during the day
Is different to the face that appears at night,
When the magical mask is taken off
And my true emotions are exposed.

Late at night, my feelings drip out of the sparkling window
To my soul. My emotions roll down my cheek,
And that in itself is a prayer to the Lord.
Even when I'm not telling anyone,
he'll always know what's on my mind,

I've been wondering,
How sad do I have to be,
For people to stop insisting,
That everything is going to be fine?
Now that sadness has been unlocked,
How long do I have to wait,
Until it is locked up once more?

I'm not suicidal

I just miss the heavenly home
I've never been to: A type of nostalgia.
Except I have experienced heaven on earth.
I'm not suicidal, though
Sometimes I wish I could vanish.
I'm not suicidal,
But I want a break from the world,
A release from the heaviness in my chest.
I'm not suicidal.
I want silence from the stress.
I'm not suicidal,
I just want to feel no emotions.
I'm not suicidal,
I want an end to the constant noise.
I'm not suicidal,
Yet I feel like I'm living to survive,
Instead of living for the Lord.
I'm not suicidal,
I don't want to die,
I'm too tired of everything,
And I just want rest as a gift from the Lord,
Which I'm struggling to receive on earth,
So no, I'm not suicidal.

Mistakes

When I was four, I dropped my plate.
I was eight when I forgot to do my homework and
Thirteen when I got my first detention.
Mistake after mistake. When will I stop?
They say forgiveness should be never ending,
Then why don't my past mistakes escape my mind?

Jesus would never do this to me.
Even though I keep making mistakes,
He still loves me—
So much that he died for me.
Why don't I move on from my past mistakes?
I say I've forgiven myself, but have I really?
I can't stop making mistakes.
The comparison game of myself to others,
And never ending pressure I place
On myself. Maybe it's my fault.

So, I started wearing a mask hoping that would fix me.
I isolated myself from reality.
I was fifteen when I hid myself from the world,
Yet that was a mistake in itself.
The increase in stress made me a mess,
And I still kept making mistakes.

Wounded

It's not the wound that hurts,
But it's the fact that the knife came
From hands I once trusted.

The sting of betrayal would be harmless
If it killed the memories along with it.
The good moments don't disappear
Even after the damage is done.

Carrying a wound you cannot keep,
Yet you can't allow your heart to close,
Creating a fine line between anger and sadness.

It's shocking when someone
You trusted so much
Turns out to be the person with the knife.

You were the reason,
For the boiling of my blood,
For the makeup dripping down my face.
You wounded me.

Rage fuels the rifle

Each topped up bullet
Increases the rage,
Until the rifle explodes, and
Releases a roaring flame.

Your minds a mess.
Your hearts in shreds,
And your friendships are fractured.
Now everyone knows about it.

The bullet-flame has been released,
And the rifle has been emptied,
Don't top up the rifle.

Escapism is a tree

It grows and gushes,
Until we can't outrun it
Anymore. Its leaves fall,
They begin to stall,
As the wind catches up to them,
And they drift.

The wind engulfs the leaves,
Becoming the fears we know as thieves,
Sprinting down the street,
Stealing all our sins and secrets.

Escapism is my tree,
Yet as the wind engulfs my leaves,
I can no longer breathe.
Each step away I take is a mistake;
Escapism is my self sabotage,
As the leaves continue to sprint down the street
Of self-sabotage
My leaves keep falling off the trees.

Addiction

Addiction is like an ocean:
I walk along its sand,
Step into the sea, and
Expose the real me.
My emotions unfold
As the blade presses to my skin,
Peeling off the layers,
Becoming one of my many slayers,
Accentuating the blood
As it flows out of my veins
And my ocean starts to drain.
The empty sea fills up with blood
Causing my mind to turn into a flood.

Hurting in silence

Silence is my loudest cry.
If you ask me if I'm okay,
I'll deny the truth: I hold a
Sadness I can't express.
Not wanting others to know what goes on
Behind closed doors.
My thoughts destroy me.
I try to ignore the internal voices,
The future fears which I cannot flee,
Yet I've settled down comfortably,
In my sadness.
Even my books cannot hear my cries,
Sadness and rage are defined
As normalities in my life.
They give me balance and healing,
I try to continue the fight,
But I am still hurting in silence.

Fitting in

When I was younger, I used to have pink wallpaper,
Now my phone background is pink.
The colour stays the same, but the reason has changed,
First my mother's choice, now the internet's.
I used to hate having my nails painted,
Now I can't go out without having them done.

Every coffee cup photo
Needs its glossy grip.
Before I used to want dark coloured nail polish,
Now I only have bright colours.
It's easier to sell sweetness than a shadow,
I learned people like me better that way,

I feel boring without jewellery,
So, I don't leave the house without it
Even though I used to hate wearing it—
The way it touched my skin was unbearable.

I grew up not wanting to fit into society.
I didn't want to be like every other girl,
Loving the colour pink and wearing jewellery,
But now I am exactly like everyone else.

I am exactly like the people I promised myself I would never become,
I don't want people to find me weird or different.
I still conform to the ways of society and
I act exactly like everyone else.

Self-sabotage

If I was an object, I would be wood.
I saw and cut at myself
More than I've known I ever could.
The carvings in the wood are textured,
An unclear piece
created by holes and betrayal.
I don't ask for help,
Leaving the pain all for myself.
The betrayal I've caused against myself
Is a result of the thoughts that plague my mind.
Every second of time,
I can't live with the idea that someone might leave,
Taking with them all my peace.
I fear that I'm the problem.
Perhaps I'm a horrible person.
Reality hits when I begin to believe these fears,
But maybe I don't deserve this friendship,
I don't *believe* I deserve it,
And you don't deserve me ruining your perfect life.
Because maybe I'm a mess
And you don't deserve my stress
Hanging over your shoulders.
Like a honeybee following you,
The potential to sting always there.
I know I'm a nice person,
But I don't want to run the risk
Of pushing you away
With my problems.
As a result of my pain and disdain,

I've become my own enemy,
With a belief I cannot change,
So, I run and hide,
Self-sabotaging so that I can make sure,
I don't cause you any more issues.

Death

Many people fear death,
But those same people,
Who are still alive,
Living through time,
In reality, have already died
The day love was ripped from their hearts.
A piece stolen and stray,
That was the day they died.
Love was their life,
But now there's nothing left for them.
No one to save them.
Nothing to live for,
Yet everything to die for.

I'm Going Deeper

Into the cycle of self-betrayal
Becoming comfortable in the confinement of my mind.
What if it's eternal?
Each step forward I try and take,
Drags me further down to the depths
Of the creation of my ache.
My legs are tied,
And I'm beginning to abide
To the demons in my mind,
Nodding along as they rewrite my truth.
Yet as much as I try,
I still continue to cry.
As I keep going deeper,
The way out becomes steeper,
And the hole which I stumbled upon,
Is now the one I try to run from.

Problems

It's not just you,
Who has problems.
Theres are millions of us,
Who are dealing with things.

But how do we deal?
We go into addiction,
Or we find distraction,
But that's not the best way out.

How do we escape,
The cruel demons of this world?
What do we do
To get out?

If we seek, we will find the Lord,
And he will always
Help us out by
Giving us redirection and protection.

It might take time,
And our quality of life might decline,
But in the end, we will be fine,
Since hope is still on the line.

Oblivious

The girl is deep in the trenches of depression.
Her heart is submerged in quicksand,
And she can't escape the extremity
Of her fluctuating feelings.

She's struggling to help herself,
Yet everyone around her
Is oblivious to it all—

Which is a good thing.
She doesn't want them to know.
Everyone's fighting their own battles,
Why should they fight hers too?

Silhouette

He felt like a silhouette,
Of the person he used to be.
His old identity erased:
A shadow fading beneath new skin.

His soul is shattered like glass.
The pieces untouchable.
The fall was fast;
A slip into the shadows he once fought,
He is no longer constructible,
Yet nobody noticed.

People reached out to pick up the pieces,
Yet it was tricky to touch them.
The glass had been fixed before,
But would they be put back together
Once more?

Branded

She was tired of her emotions.
So, she wore a mask branded with smiles.
It was a new mask,
That bottled up all her thoughts and feelings,
Keeping them safe inside.
She only took it off when she could hide.
Why should anyone care,
When there's no valid reason to wear
this eraser of emotions?
Everyone's tired of their own feelings.
Each person has a situation that they're dealing with,
So, maybe it's best if she keeps her feelings to herself—
Except for God.
She'll tell him how she feels,
She'll rely on him to keep her out of hell on earth
So that one day
She'll finally be able to take off this mask
And find out what heaven on earth feels like.

Living to survive

"You'll survive," they say,
As I walk out of the church doors.
"You'll be okay," I'm told.

I've lost someone
And those are the only comforting words
They can muster.
I know that in time I'll learn
To live with the grief,

To survive the cards I've been dealt.
I'll pick up the pieces of my shattered glass,
And I'll live life as I used to,
Except I won't hear your voice.
I can't have any more hugs from you,
Yet that's not my choice.

Each day is another passing minute of being eaten alive,
Hardly being able to survive.
People will think I'm happy once more,
Yet deep down in my core,
I know that I'm just living to survive.

My plans

God had to ruin my plans,
Before they ruined me.
My plans were small,
Yet they had a big chance breaking down:
I planned for love, but his hand
Shifted, and tore the tides apart.

If they had worked,
They would've hurt me,
And I would have had to heal,
From something that wasn't in God's plan for me.

When we didn't get together,
I thought it was all over.
I questioned the point of a life
With no purpose.

My care for him was like a seed in a desert,
I expected it to grow into a garden.
As soon as it began to grow,
Suddenly it died.
It had a lack of nourishment.

God had to ruin my plans,
Before they ruined me.

Hate

Hatred is the coward's revenge for being intimidated.
                — *George Bernard Shaw*

There's a Demon Living In my mind

He lives there rent free
Leaving and entering as he pleases.

He replays my memories and tells me stories.
He tells me my makeup is ugly, and that my outfit looks bad.
My hair doesn't look good, he tells me,
And that the way my voice sounds isn't nice.

Do people at church fight this battle too?
Maybe it's spiritual warfare.
Do other people fight these demons,

The kind that make you doubt yourself,
And tell you false truths,
The ones that tell you what to do?

Perhaps that's why I don't hear God's voice,
Because Satan is whispering in my mind,
And even though his voice is quiet it's all I can hear.

I wonder when this demon will leave.
The answer is probably never.
Why would he leave when he's in control?

Proof of my hate for you

You're everywhere,
You haunt me every second of the day.
I shut the door of our friendship months ago,
But your ghost follows me from the past.

Through doors, walls, books, and meals,
You're everywhere.
Some might say this is proof of my love for you;
They would be correct.

Yet the love which I once had
Is now lost, and
The only thing here is hate.
Like a bag of blood had burst on my kitchen floor.
The crumbs of your character call me.

Was your life goal to put me in my grave then grieve?
You stripped me of many friendships.
You said I'd get nowhere in life.
Your manipulation was as simple as a sigh in silence.

The day you called me dumb was the day I died.
My soul lives eternally through my writing,
And your day of death is soon.
The day I release my poetry book is the day you die,
This might just be proof of my hate for you.

Guilt

When a person feels guilt,
It's supposed to be because of a wrong they have committed.
Yet I haven't done anything,
So why do a feel this way?

Guilt is like a guitar,
Its strings are played powerfully.
I'm no longer in control;
I'm not the one playing them.
The instrument follows me around.
It's attached to my back
Like a part of my skin.

Guilt is like a hand.
It grips onto my throat
Choking me until
I'm left gasping for air.

If guilt was a person,
He would hate me.
Guilt would want me dead,
But he wouldn't make it easy.
He'd want it to hurt,

Not just me,
But everyone around me.
He would want people to burn alive.
I feel so guilty,
Yet I haven't committed an inhumane act.

Why do I feel guilty?

I am the demon

If I was to kill someone,
I'd make it look like suicide.
If I was to kill someone,
It would be me.

I'd murder the demon inside me.
Stabbing the knife into my chest,
The blood would be on my hands,
And I'd wonder who caused this.

When in reality,
The demon is sitting
right in front of me:
The addiction,
The anxiety,

Is all because of me.
In the mirror,
I see the demon
Is a spitting image of myself.

You ruined me

You carried me to the heavens,
Then decided to drop me to hell in seconds.
They say no one's perfect,
But I really thought you were the one.
I believed the lies,
Trusted your disguise.
The sting of your betrayal
Would be harmless
If it killed my love for you along with it.
My heart was finally healing,
And before you'd even started the teasing,
You ripped it right out of my chest.
Blood poured out of my body,
As if I was a nobody.
You ruined me at my best,
Yet your heart was still in your chest,
I was delusional and
The love I saw was welcoming.
I was blinded by who I thought you were,
And shattered by the truth of who you are.
Laughing after you dropped me in hell,
Does that ring a bell?
You blamed me,
But perhaps you were the problem.
You broke the mirror I used to see myself,
The broken shards cut into my skin,
You ruined me.

Pink

When I was younger, I hated the colour pink.
Everyone did.
We all hated how pink was a symbol of womanhood,
Not that we hated being women,
Just that women were perceived as weak,
And pretty.

"Pretty girls love pink," they said,
But I didn't want to just be seen for being pretty.
The girls that express their love for pink are haters.
Girls support girls,
Until one girl becomes a bully.

Pink is a synonym of femininity.
I like pink, but I hate wearing dresses.
The meaning of flowers in pink,
Is friendship,
Yet the real-life representation is elegance.

Why do some colours represent girls,
But some only represent boys?
Why do stereotypes exist?
So, yes, I do like pink,
But I don't tell anyone that.

What was once the truth

If I had called you out, what would've happened?
I know one thing for sure,
I would not have been seen as right.

You would've added lies to what was once the truth,
To make yourself be seen as the good guy.
Everything bad you've done,
Would be seen as a lie and

I would be the bad guy.
That's why,
I protected my peace,
And I never called you out.

Goodbye

I finally had the courage to say goodbye.
You might call it selfish,
But I call it protecting my peace.

I'll cherish our memories together,
But I'll also feel bitter towards the bad moments.
Each memory that we shared will always be remembered.

You're probably wondering why.
If you want to know,
All you have to think about is every argument you started,

And you'll realise that how you treated me
Was unfair. Or maybe you'll gaslight yourself,
Maybe you justify your actions.
Deep down you know that what you did was wrong,
Or at least, I hope you do.
So, this is my goodbye.

Comparison is the Thief of Joy

You look at your work and feel satisfied.
Satisfaction is like an orange.
You love oranges,
But as soon as you compare it,
To a dragon fruit, something more unique,
You no longer feel satisfied.

Pay attention to your own work.
You will be satisfied with this beautiful piece of creativity.
You'll be joyful,
But as soon as you compare,

The thief begins his work,
And takes away your joy.

Cigarette

"Don't be a cigarette," You're told.
Even though you know you're the opposite of that,
You continue to wonder what this means.

Don't let people
Treat you like a cigarette,
Use you as a second option,
Like you have no value.
You're not a keepsake, just a passing flame,
They don't treat you like you're worth,
Use you when they're bored,
Then step on you when they're done
And destroy you.

They use you until you can no longer take it.
Until you snap at them,
And leave then find people who know your worth.
No one values you beyond the burn.
They act like they care,
But, in reality, they don't.
They've used up the whole cigarette,
And all that's left is the ashes.

Locked and Loaded

Your gun is locked and loaded,
Yet the truth has already exploded.
You're a murderer.
You killed the relationship we used to have.
The gun was loaded with hatred,
Reality no longer gated,
And now our friendship has imploded.
It was dead a long time ago.
Not a single conversation,
As I walk past you,
You've become a stranger to me.
Your laughter echoes,
As I hear you laugh with a different person.
You've unlocked a new me,
Now, my gun is locked and loaded.

Suffocation

Each word exiting your mouth,
Brings me closer to suffocation.
You're causing my elimination.
I don't hate you,
But you've lost all my respect,
You don't realise how your words have an effect.
There's a reason why I keep it all inside.
I'm trying to hide
The feelings which are yet to subside.
You've created a mess.
Is this a test
To see if I'm good enough,
Or have you got nothing left?
Every word spewing out of your mouth
Is hate. Was this a mistake?
It seems like you want me to suffocate.

Not really proud

It takes silence and space,
For me to realise,
That you're proud of her, aren't you?
But can't you be proud of me too?
I've slowed down my pace,
So that perhaps I can taste
What it's like to be proud of my creations.
Yet, the more you stay quiet,
The more I realise
I hate the way
Your lack of pride ruins my day.
I begin to put up my defence
Against your power.
As my tears begin to dispense,
I lock the gate
Not allowing you to see the great
Façade which I've put on.
Your proud of her,
But blind to all I'm worth.
As a new version of me is born
You silently mourn
The grades which I could've had,
And my failures, which have been bad.
Maybe all I need is silence and space.

God says

I am fearfully and wonderfully made,
But how can that be true if I don't believe it about myself?
We are told to believe everything that comes out of the mouth
Of the Lord, which I do— except for that.
How can I be fearfully and wonderfully made,
If I am completely flawed inside and out?
Satan tells me that I'm a horrible person.
God's image of me is much better than the starter of sins.
Perhaps it's a good thing that I don't believe I'm fearfully and wonderfully made,
Deeply valued and crafted with care and intention.
Because if I did would I be committing another sin?
Would that be prideful?

The Lord's image of me is lovely,
But my image of me isn't.
He sees me as kind, creative, and curious,
Self-image is
Something that plays in your mind,
Every passing second.
Is it me that struggles with self-image,
Or is it Sly Satan giving me ideas?
Maybe that's a question for another day,
After all, God says I'm fearfully and wonderfully made.

Society pretty

When I was eight, I wondered why my mum wore makeup.
She told me it was to look pretty,
But I thought she was already.

When I was eleven,
I saw other girls wearing full faces of makeup,
But I only wanted to wear a minimal amount.

When I was fifteen,
I started experimenting with outfits,
Chasing fashion trends and styles,
I did it to fit into society's version of pretty.

Now I'm seventeen,
And I follow the trends
Of outfits and makeup.
Because if I don't then surely,
I won't fit in, right?

Society's standard of pretty changes continuously
And we follow along with it
Closing the door to any outfits we used to wear before,
No longer bothered to wilfully explore.

Don't take it personally

I could never hate you,
Not as much as I hate that slithery snake:

The snake who started sin,
Who sends us torment,
The one who causes disagreements.

The being who was so prideful,
That he used his free will wrongly.
So much that he wanted to be better than God.

So, if it seems like I hate you,
Don't take it personally,
Because I could never hate you,
At least not as much as I hate Satan.

I don't trust happiness

Happiness is a good thing,
Until you feel it chipping away at you one day at a time.
You feel it slowly turning into anger,
Until it becomes sadness.
Happiness often leads to betrayal,
It's like a friend who lies,
Just to keep you lingering little longer.
It feels like life-long lasting,
Until it's gone, like you'd never known it,
And now your good friend happiness has been obliterated.
Next time you feel happy,
Remember how happiness has hurt you,
When you test the waters, to see how happy you can get,
Play it safe, and remember why I've told you,
No, I don't trust happiness.
Each time you feel happy,
Know that it won't last forever,
You'll look back in the future
Remembering how happy you were,
And wonder,
"Where has my happiness gone?"

Do I hate myself?

Or am I just guessing the aim of the card game?
Am I being played by the ultimate player?

Is Satan making me believe that I hate myself,
When that's not really true?
Perhaps he's adding more cards filled with lies to my deck.

It feels like no matter what I do,
I'm letting everyone down,
Including myself.
I'm continuing to add cards labelled F to my pile.

So, what is really true?
Do I really hate myself and
Am I letting people down,
Or do my cards actually belong in Satan's deck?

Or is everything just one big lie?
What is the truth?

Manipulator

Everything was perfect.
At first we were good friends,
We had fun together,
And I enjoyed your company.
You supported me through the hard times,
And I accept that you were there for me.
I'm grateful for that,

But then you turned against me.
We began to argue,
I felt isolated. You lied
To our other friends about me,
Like a prime minister would do,
To gain support and trust,
When in reality, it was all built upon a lie.

Everything others knew about me was erased.
My personality, my actions, and my passions,
You made me into a new person,
And you had changed.
I no longer knew the person I was once friends with.
You might have had insecurities,
But that doesn't mean you had to give me some too.
You are a manipulator,
And I'm so glad

That I did pick up your qualities
Of manipulation and intimation
By staying friends with you.

Friendships always have the honeymoon phase,
Where a person's true self is hidden,

Until you can see it in plain sight.
Then, so will everyone else.
Unless you're a manipulator,
Then your hands are covered in blood,
Not mine.

Insane

I am not insane,
I just have a lot to gain
Without your disdain
Causing my pain.
Perhaps you're insane
For being so obsessed,
Which you repressed
Through hatred and false accusations.
Is my time being wasted,
As you taunt and flaunt
All the information you've acquired,
When really perhaps I'm being admired?
You still continue to haunt,
Spilling secrets about my life,
Yet now I'm the one with the knife.

Closed eyes

I finally opened my eyes
Taking off the disguise
That covered my mind.
My closed eyes hid the truth
About you.
You're no longer kind,
And we don't have that bind
Which used to attach us together.
Now I've moved on forever,
Unlocked the truth behind the
Glimmer in your eyes.
You wanted my demise,
Yet now I arise.
You're beginning to shrink,
As if it all happened in a blink.
My eyes have snapped open,
The angels have spoken,
The truth about you
Has ripped the group apart,
Shredding us at heart,
Along with what was once a lively personality too.

Control

I kept asking myself,
What changed?
What information did you gain,
To cause me to become an outcast?
All so fast,
Before you'd discovered the facts,
You became someone I wanted to bypass.
Yet, you let me back in,
Making me think I'd win,
When really it was all a part of your plan.
You'd ended my lifespan,
Entering with your clan,
To intimidate
And manipulate.
That's when I realised,
You didn't want to fight.
You did it out of spite,
Craving control,
Wanting to parole.
I learnt that people turn to hate
When they can no longer control you.

A Sword is a Weapon of War

Allowing me to explore
All your lore,
Shedding some light,
Causing you to put up a fight,
Arguing with all your might.
The sword stabs my chest,
Bleeding out until my death,
And you'll no longer rest.
You'll stay in the fiery pits of hell,
Locked in your cell.
Now I've stolen your sword,
And earned you a place in the furnace,
Ending your service
And saving others from the sickness,
Of dread, that you can no longer spread.
Your sword was once a weapon of war,
But now that I've taken it,
You'll no longer be able to claw
At my face,
Making our friendship look like a mistake.

To be loved by a writer

"Oh, to be loved by," a writer,
That's all people say,
But what they really want is
Someone to sit down, write, in the middle of May,
A masterpiece to display.
I become the pen which you move along the paper
Just to say goodbye to later,
The piece of paper scrunched into a ball,
As if it was always ever so small.
The person which you once knew evaporates,
Unlike you,
Every fibre of your being becomes words on a page,
And you no longer age.
The last part of your personality I ever saw,
Becomes all you live for.

Now that I've written yours,
Who holds the pen that writes my story?

The hatred coming out of the characters—
Which I created based on you—
The destruction of their calluses,
My hatred for you showing through those too.
Do you really want to be loved by a writer,
Or do you just want the people to love you?

Fame is just a game

Ordinary people continue to play,
Placing more cards down from the deck,
Adding more money from our pockets to their pay checks,
Each watch and comment another pound
Into the ground
We live on.
Just to let them pawn,
For just one more pound.
Another listen, another like,
So, their dreams will come to light.
Yet, we're working all day and all night,
Praying that the total will suffice.
It's just enough to feed our families,
Yet, they're earning billions, and
Slow to donate just one million.
When you're in the grave the crowd cries,
Yet, those children are still starving with
Their parents working till their deaths while
You've paid millions for a five second space trip
Which could've saved those children's lives.
Just a pound from your pocket
Could've launched donations like a rocket.
It's all just a flicker in the dark to you.
You turn a blind eye
Watching as parents cry,
Yet you still continue to deny,
The people who died
Living in a war
That you could've paused,

All this for fame,
But what did you really gain?

Hollow

Don't fill the hollow spaces in your heart with people who are empty. -Indigo Storm

Devils' waters

The waves arrive.
I didn't leave,
I couldn't rise,
You gave me no choice.
I was trapped in the
deep depths of the ocean—
This dark ocean—
There was no way out.
Will I be stuck here forever
Until my flesh rots,
My voice fades away,
My heart stops,
And my bones drop?

I keep telling you I'm tired,
But you won't let me go.
Perhaps my bones will turn to dust,
Just like my soul,
Which you stole.
All that's left of me,
Is my favourite chair,
The one you made me sit on,
The place where you
Began to take the pieces
I thought only belonged to me.

I've come to realise,
The ocean didn't belong to God.
This wasn't a trial or a tribulation,

It was a trick from Satan
And these were the devils' waters.

Betrayal

How did Jesus feel when he was betrayed by Judas?
A choice that caused an atmosphere of dullness
As the veil was torn from top to bottom and
All sin was forgotten.
Jesus welcomed Judas into the group with open arms,
Yet he was still harmed,
And Judas didn't think to be alarmed as if
There would be no repercussions.
How did he continue loving Judas,
Even though he knew he'd be killed?
Betrayal is like a knife through the chest,
Yet Jesus felt it while nailed to the cross.
Judas did what would benefit him best,
Without leaving a thought for his Lord.
Even after Peter had pulled up a sword,
Splitting the Roman soldier's ear,
Jesus healed the soldier, no matter his fate,
Knowing that it had already been served to him on a plate.
The suffering that he would endure,
Was all so that we could eternally explore
His love forever.
What if there was no betrayal?
What if Judas had stayed loyal,
Ignored the temptations,
Sticking to Jesus' expectations?
Betrayal alters dreams,
A whispered secret which
Twists your life,
Stabbing you in the chest like a knife.
Have you ever betrayed a friend who was like a brother?

Acceptance is my Muse

One which I have started to abuse,

The once white canvas is now underpainted in black,

I've tried to approve what you did to me,

With splashes of blue,

But I am still yet to see

A painted beach staring back at me.

I thought it didn't affect me anymore,

Yet that thought cannot be true,

My hands are tainted in yellow,

I wish I could acknowledge it:

My pain and hurt

Comes up at the rise of night and

I try to push it down nice and tight. Yet, no matter how hard I fight,

Reality comes to light

Shades of red still show up in the sunset

I have started to recognise

That I will have to accept what you put me through,

And move on.

Dicentra

A wounded heart on every vine,
Just like you've hurt mine,
Yet you're still oh so divine,
Your beauty surpasses every piece of art.
A string of hearts.
Your disconnection sends darts
Right through mine.
My bleeding drops of love
Cover me, unable to be sent your way.
I live in the garden where lost lovers part.
You still have my heart.
My tears are like love unspoken,
And I'm still heartbroken with
My love forever stolen.

Stranger

Each night I cry,
As I think about you,
And what you put me through.
Yet, I feel conflicted
When I reminisce about the small
and good times we had.

I miss the you that I used to know,
And I hate the person who's now a
Stranger to me.
What happened to you?
Why did you change?

I will forever question,
Why you did this to me.
Is there something I can't see,
Or is the issue only between you and me,
Rather than the parade of people
Who we used to know?
Yet after all you put me through,
You're no longer my friend,
And I'm a stranger to you.

So, now, each night
When I lay down,
I'll no longer think of you.
Instead, I'll think of the blessing,
Of you being taken from me,
The cut off which I caused,

As I remember that I'm a stranger to you,
Because of what you did to me.

Fear

When I was a child, I was afraid of the dark.
I remember turning off the lights before running to my room.
Time has passed since then and I'm no longer afraid of the dark.
My fears go deeper than the here and the now,
I'm afraid of healing from my past and what awaits me in the future.

Now, I fear the night, but it's not because of the dark, it's because of my mind.
The battles that take place and the memories that resurface.
Is it Satan attacking my mind, or is it God telling me that I need healing?
The expected replay of the past in my mind
Is like a trailer for a movie, yet so real and vivid.

Fear is a powerful emotion. It can stop us from gaining so much.
Yet, it can also save us from risk taking and pain.
We are told to overcome fear, but will it be worth it?

Attachment

Attachment is sweet but sticky,
Clinging to the person like there's no other option.
Is attachment a bad thing?
I'm attached to the way you speak.
I cling to your words like honey sticks to a bee.
I stick to your sweetness like water sticks to the sand.
Your personality is bittersweet:
One minute you're kind and generous,
Another you're annoyed and irritable.
Finding someone that makes me happy
Is a scary thing.
I give you all of my attention and
How you treat me begins to affect my mood.
You take control over my emotions
Without knowing you've even done it.
The three days that you haven't spoke to me
Become days of deep depression.
I want to make it stop,
But how can I stop being attached
To someone that I have so much love for?

Anxiety

Anxiety: I hate her so much,
But it's impossible to get rid of her.
She clings to me like mud sticks to my shoes.
I wash her off for the hour, until she returns.
She's stuck with me for a while now.
She won't leave me alone.
She's been with me for a few years and
Some might say she's looking out for me,
But I think differently.
She ruins every experience that I have.
She makes me feel sick to my stomach.
I don't want to be friends with her,
But she won't leave me alone.
She stays with me during the good and the bad.
She hugs me tightly all the time.
When she's with me I feel like I can't move.
"Leave me alone," I tell her,
But she doesn't listen.
So, I suppose I'm stuck with her forever.
I have lots of friends,
But she makes me feel so alone, like I have no one.
She suffocates me,
My best friend is anxiety.

Denial

Denial is the refusal of acceptance.
It's the devil's playground of defiance,
Abducting me from a fun place and
Putting me in a maze.
The monster stood in front of me,
I kept telling myself it was just a dream,
But I know what that really means:
Not wanting to face the truth.
When the mind-monsters return,
Affecting my internal world,
Denial is my go-to,
Helping me to ignore you,
The removal of temporary pain,
Ignoring the reality of facing my fears.

Ghosted

When people are ghosted, they usually feel hate.
Yet, my feelings for you are anything but that—
They're the opposite.
All I feel for you is love and loss.

My feelings for you are like a honey-hoarding bee,
The droplets of dew which are left behind as you leave,
are slightly too much for me to proceed.

I would like to argue that hate is better than love,
Especially when a relationship is ending,
But I didn't get that luxury this time.

Instead, I'm waiting for you,
And I cherish the moment when you come back to me
Because you haven't made one mistake.
You're kind, caring, and creative,

And that's your mistake.
You're so perfect that I can't help but speak to you
As soon as you come right back to me.

I feel lost without you,
Like you've stolen a section of my soul,
And I can't seem to regain or retain it
Anywhere else.

Maybe that's why I'm in despair and desperation,
For the bee to come buzzing back,
Just to linger then leave.

Do I trust you?

I don't want friends who make me question
Whether we are really friends
Because that what I used to have.
I want true friendships.
My trust has been fractured,
And I don't know if it can be restored.
No amount of good friendships can repair the damage.
It has taken a lot of pain to break my heart.
With my shattered heart, along went my trust.
Friendships might seem like they've healed but have they really?

Now I have a good friend
And I'm still struggling to trust,
But I promised myself I would be different.
I vowed to myself that I would trust *you*.

However, I'm struggling to do exactly that.
It's hard to do what I used to be so good at doing.
Holding constant fear that it's going to be over,
Thanks to her
I wonder to myself, do I trust you?

Secrets

Secrets are like seeds in a plant pot
Separate from all the other plants
Roaming around the garden.

They want to be known,
Yet they're unable to be shown.
The roots spread

Until the flower surfaces,
But something stops the petals
From expanding.

They seem pale against the dark,
A flower which forgot how to absorb the sun.
No breath of green runs through its roots,

Only pale petals are what's seen.
They're half uprooted,
Yet they cling to the soil.

Secrets stay hidden.
The buds hold their breath,
And the plants stay stuck in the pot.

Silver

Everyone wants silver,
Silver jewellery,
Silver coloured pens,
Silver starry sky.

But no one wanted silver as much as Judas did.
We say, *I'd do anything to get that,*
But would we really?
Probably not.

Judas did worse than that.
He sold a whole person,
And not just any person,
The king of the heavenly world.

Not just any king,
The saviour of the world.
He sold King Jesus,
Jesus of Nazareth.

The same Jesus
Who welcomed him with open arms.
The same Jesus who was nothing but kind to him.
My heart breaks for Jesus Christ

I definitely wouldn't sell out anyone,
For some silver.

Tears

Tears are like leaves:
Different types and colours.
Sometimes leaves fall:
They don't stay on branches forever.

There are different reasons to cry:
For joy, sadness, or laughter.
A lot of the time people don't cry,

Tears taste salty
Just like the sea:
The wide endless ocean.
When we'll see the ocean next is unknown.

We need water to live,
Yet if there's too much of it
We will drown.

Our bodies are over 50% water,
Yet my face is basically 100% water
With how much I cry. But it is a release

Of emotions. Tears can heal;
It's healthy to cry.
Everyone has tears sometimes.

Walking away

The hardest part about walking away from someone
Isn't the walking away,
It's the realisation that no matter how slow you walk,
They'll never chase after you.
You fight for the person many more times than you should.
You give them lots of opportunities
To make things right,
Yet nothing changes.
Walking away isn't weak,
It requires strength.
I don't need other people to realise
How much I'm worth, or my value,
As much as I should realise it on my own.
Walking away isn't a loss,
It's a gain of my own self-respect.
I finally valued myself again.
So, I chose to fight for myself
And I walked away.

Another life

Maybe there was another life where we never broke apart,
Where we weren't pushing to make things right.
A world where I wasn't left wondering and overthinking
About how we can have a happy life.
A world where I realised that the best thing for me would be to walk away.
A world where you weren't uncertain about what you really wanted.

I'm no longer living in a world of uncertainty and fun
Because I've already tried that,
And it's what led me to how much worse my life is now.
Maybe in another life I won't be imprisoned in a cage
Locked up with monsters which haunt my nights and days.
Perhaps it's me in this life who's causing all the problems and pain.
The reality we are living in is the one where you didn't choose me.
Maybe in the next one you will—
In another life.

Haunted

I'm haunted by you,
By the things you said, and the comments you made.
Every time I look at my patchy makeup,
I realise that's something you would've commented on.
On my bad hair days, I think about what you would've said.

Each rude and irrelevant thing you've ever said to me
Comes back to haunt me every day.
Why does it feel like a ghost is following me
Throughout the days and weeks of my life
Even though you're still alive?

My life is a mess.
It feels like you're the reason
That this mess started.

Every sentence you've ever said
Follows me around and
Your words are my shadow.
It seems like your ghost is following me,
Even though you're still alive.
How can that be?
Why are you haunting me?

Homesick

She feels homesick.
How is that possible
When she's never visited that home?
For some people home is a person
Or maybe it's a place.
For her, it's a specific space
That we can't reach in the physical realm.
When people ask her why she wants the rapture to happen,
She tells them it's because she hates earth,
Which is partly true,
But the full truth is that she misses that place
Which one day will be her home.
She feels nostalgic towards this place,
She feels hiraeth for heaven.
She feels homesick.

The backup friend

I look nothing like the girl you liked.
I don't have straight, long, blond hair like she does.
Instead, I have short brown curls.
I stay up at night
Thinking about what I could do to make you like me.
I hid part of myself because you told me to.
You told me my hobbies were embarrassing
So, I hid them away.
You'd only hang out with me when she wasn't there.
It made me feel special,
Like I had a good friend.
For a short time, you'd make me feel like the first choice.
But then when she'd come back, I was the backup friend.
This cycle was on repeat:
The same feeling of disappointment and distaste
When I realised that I was a filler option.
As much as I wanted to be wrong, I always knew the truth.
I was the backup friend.

Society's cell

I'm a fake version of myself.
"Straighten your hair— no, keep your curls."
I'm living in stealth
Tiptoeing around society's cell.
There's overconsumption everywhere you look.
Where has real beauty been taken?
My wishes cannot be shaken.
Society created a system,
Where you have to look a certain way
Or else you can no longer stay.
The locked door stops me.
As much as I hate the matrix
I don't want to admit
I do like putting on makeup.
The small things in this world
Play a part in my life,
Yet the key to my locked cell
Belongs to the higher ups.
Only they will ever be able to tell
What more they can sell
To keep me to stay.
Even if I do unlock the door,
I will no longer be able to escape the floor,
And exit the real world.
I will never be able to create a reality
Which doesn't exist.
I will always be stuck in society's cell.

Cannot feel any rest

A gaping hole exists in my chest.
I cannot feel any rest.
Beginning to take my last breath,
My heart implodes,
Unable to physically explode.
No longer feeling any pain
Or disdain,
On the day of my funeral,
People will remember me at my best,
Not knowing that I had already taken my rest
Years ago.
My words so shallow,
Not living up to what I promise.
The darkness taking over,
Cracking jokes and creating ideas,
All just until the sun rises,
And hopefully you don't notice I'm gone.
People will begin to morn,
Not noticing that's something which should've been done long ago
Because that gaping hole in my chest
Began to expand,
And I could not feel any rest.

Difficult to love

I am difficult to love.
Hollow and hard around the edge:
The thick walls around my heart
Are hard to knock down.
When someone is brave enough,
To start hammering at my walls,
I give up before they can fully begin.
I don't let them in,
Fearing that they'll leave,
A truth which has happened multiple times.
I know it's true,
Because if I was easy to love,
Then why would everyone end up leaving?

Museum of memories

My mind is a museum of memories:
I want to forget each action and every reaction,
The moments of dissatisfaction.
As I grew, so did my heart:
My bleeding heart blossomed
Blooming like art.
Written details below my artifacts:
Each line another decrease in my energy.
With it, out came the problems
From its cracking and fracturing,
Yet it dissociates from me.
Every letter, another page erased,
Filled with a person who
Walked in and passed by.
Every comma and semi colon written with their ink,
Until my life stopped fitting their vibe.
People move on as I try not to cry.
Ignoring my emotions—
I don't feel them passing,
My hearts artefacts are
Hardly holding it together.
My pain is put on as a display for others
To see that I can't hold on any longer,
Yet they still don't understand.
Hearing my name come out of their lips
Makes me stay, just for them.
If they can't see my pain,
Maybe they'll start to see me.
Perhaps I won't just be a person they put up with.

They can finally start to like me,
So, my heart continues to be a museum of memories.

Acknowledgements

I would like to thank my family, as well as my friends from church, for encouraging me to write this book, and for always believing in me throughout the hard times in my life. I would also like to thank the people in church who are given the wisdom to answer any questions that I have and who make me feel like I'm not a burden to talk to. I am so grateful to be blessed by God, who has given me these beautiful and amazing people. I would also like to thank my readers. I wouldn't have been able to publish this book without you, so thank you. I also want to thank Luminary Publishing House for helping me through this process and for the kindness you have shown.

Lastly, I would like to thank the being who is the first and the last [Revelation 22:13]. I want to thank my Lord and saviour, Jesus Christ. You might not believe that he is God, you might have even had a bad experience with religious people, but remember, even Jesus himself had bad experiences with religious people. Those same religious people are the ones who crucified him on a cross and killed him. True Christianity is a relationship with Jesus, NOT religion.

My Testimony

I grew up in a Christian household. We went to church every Sunday, and I read the bible occasionally, but I never knew Jesus on a personal level. When I was fourteen, my mental health began to suffer, and I felt unmotivated towards everything in life. I had no idea what my purpose was, and I hid how I felt from everyone. I began to seek temporary relief from these burdens, which is when I began to self-harm. There was a time when it got so bad that it was a daily addiction. Throughout this time, I still believed in God, but I was not seeking him, and I had no idea what to do. I told my friend Rachael about how I felt, and she helped me as best she could. When my mum found out about it, she was upset for me, and I knew she had been praying for me to have freedom from my struggles. Maybe you've heard similar stories to this before, about how God has helped people who have had bad mental health, but that wasn't all. At the same time as this, I dealt with judgment about past choices.

At the time, the youth group I attended was going for a few days away for a conference. On the first evening meeting, the person speaking said that she knew that someone in the room had self-harm scars. Only my friend Rachael knew about this, and I trusted that she didn't tell this youth leader about my self-harm. In this moment, I knew that God was the one who told her this. Later that night, this same youth leader sat with me, and she told me that I had a wall that I needed to name so I could break it down. I knew that this wall was self-harm, and my struggles with mental health as a whole. Later in the conference, I had a conversation with this youth leader again, and I figured out God had also told her that I dealt with judgment about past choices, and that this was not wrong.

A day later, God had revealed to me that I was like a pigeon. This confused me at first, but I discovered pigeons always return to their original homes. I thought I would go to hell, but this was God telling me that I would return to him in heaven when my time came.

A few months after this, I began to rebuild my relationship with Christ, and I was set free from bad mental health. I got baptised on the same day as Rachael. The heavenly and joyful feeling that came over me when I was in the baptism pool was honestly beautiful, and I've never experienced anything like it.

However, about a year afterwards, there was a short period of time, about a week, where I felt my bad mental health coming back again. I refused to give in to the temptation to self-harm and the urge to relapse. Instead, what I began to do was to read my bible as soon as I woke up, and to listen to worship music before I went to sleep (or whenever I felt down). This has been a great method in my healing journey.

I am so grateful for how far the Lord has brought me through my journey of faith and in life, and I am still continuing to go through my healing journey. This is hard, but I know that I will come out on the other side much more joyful than when I entered, instead of getting the temporary feeling of happiness from things that are only temporary.

Hard times can still come even after the deliverance from God, but he will always take you through them. These experiences helped me learn how to deal with them better each time. I learn new skills on every bump in my journey, which helps make the recovery process faster.

My sadness has shown me that I need saving. I now appreciate the beauty of life, and I value myself more than ever because I know that my worth comes from Jesus. I pray that God can help you to do the same, and I hope my testimony shows that God can do the same for you. God bless you!

"The Lord bless you and keep you; the Lord make his face shine on you and be gracious to you; the Lord turn his face toward you and give you peace."

– Numbers 6:24-26

Author Bio

Lily Isaac is a teen poet and debut author based in England. Of Egyptian heritage and Arabic descent, she brings a unique cultural and emotional lens to her writing. Her journey into poetry began during a deeply challenging time in her life, when words became a refuge and a way to process pain, fear, and identity struggles. What started as a coping mechanism evolved into a powerful creative outlet, and ultimately, a voice for others who feel unseen or unheard.

Her work is rooted in lived experience, drawing from personal battles with mental health, heartache, and the complexities of growing up. Through her poetry, she aims to remind readers that they are not alone, that their emotions are valid, and that connection can be found even in the darkest moments.

This debut collection is a testament to resilience, vulnerability, and the healing power of expression. Lily writes not to impress, but to offer comfort, solidarity, and hope to anyone who needs it.